Landon Donovan

Arturo Contró

English translation: Megan Benson

PowerKiDS press™

Editorial Buenas Letras™

New York

Published in 2008 by The Rosen Publishing Group, Inc.
29 East 21st Street, New York, NY 10010

First Edition
Book Design: Nelson Sa

Cataloging Data

Contró, Arturo, 1967-
    Landon Donovan / Arturo Contró; English translation: Megan Benson — 1st ed.
        p.cm. – (World Soccer Stars / Estrellas del fútbol mundial)
    Includes Index.
    ISBN: 978-1-4042-7666-6
    1. Donovan, Landon–Juvenile literature. 2. Soccer players–Biography–Juvenile
literature. 3. Spanish-language materials.

Manufactured in the United States of America

Photo Credits: Cover (left) © Paul J. Richards/Getty Images; cover (right) © Stephen Dunn/Getty Images; p. 5 © Jonathan Ferrey/Getty Images; pp. 7, 21 © Brian Bahr/ Getty Images; p. 9 © Alex Livesey/Getty Images; p. 11 © Phil Walter/Getty Images; pp. 13, 15 © Jonathan Ferrey/Getty Images; pp. 17, 19 © Shaun Botterill/Getty Images.

Contents

1 Meet Landon Donovan   **4**

2 Top Scorer   **10**

3 Donovan's Fans   **18**

Glossary   **22**

Resources   **23**

Index   **24**

Contenido

1 Conoce a Landon Donovan   **4**

2 Donovan goleador   **10**

3 Los admiradores de Donovan   **18**

Glosario   **22**

Recursos   **23**

Índice   **24**

Landon Donovan is one of the most famous soccer players in the United States. Donovan was born on March 4, 1982, in Ontario, California.

Landon Donovan es uno de los futbolistas más famosos de los Estados Unidos. Landon nació el 4 de marzo de 1982, en Ontario, California.

5

When Donovan was six years old, he told his mother that he wanted to be a soccer player. On his first game with a children's team, he scored seven goals.

Cuando Donovan tenía 6 años de edad, le dijo a su mamá que quería ser jugador de fútbol. En su primer partido con un equipo infantil, Landon anotó 7 goles.

When he was 16, Donovan became a **professional** player, with the team Bayer Leverkusen, in Germany.

A los 16 años, Donovan empezó a jugar como **profesional** en el equipo Bayer Leverkusen de Alemania.

In 1999, Donovan played on the U.S. team in the U-17 **World Cup**. This is the World Cup for players younger than 17. Donovan was named the best player in that cup.

En 1999, Donovan jugó con los Estados Unidos el Mundial sub-17. Esta es la **Copa del Mundo** para jugadores menores de 17 años. Donovan fue nombrado Mejor Jugador de la copa.

11

Donovan is one of the best **scorers** in the **MLS**. He played for the San Jose Earthquakes from 2001 to 2004. Donovan scored 42 goals with the Earthquakes.

Donovan es uno de los mejores **goleadores** de la **MLS**. Donovan jugó con el San José Earthquakes, de 2001 a 2004. Donovan anotó 42 goles con los Earthquakes.

13

In 2005, Donovan joined the team Los Angeles Galaxy. Donovan helped the Galaxy win the MLS championship that year.

En 2005, Donovan se unió al equipo de Los Ángeles Galaxy. Aquel año, Donovan ayudó al Galaxy a ganar el campeonato de la MLS.

Many people think that Donovan is the best American soccer player in history. Donovan has scored more than 30 goals for the U.S. soccer team.

Muchas personas piensan que Donovan es el mejor jugador de fútbol de la historia de los Estados Unidos. Donovan ha anotado más de 30 goles con la selección de Estados Unidos.

Donovan is famous for his speed. He moves quickly with the ball and scores many goals.

Donovan es famoso por su gran velocidad. Donovan se mueve muy rápido con el balón y anota muchos goles.

Landon Donovan has many fans. In 2002, he visited American troops in South Korea. Donovan signed soccer balls and photographs.

Landon Donovan tiene muchos seguidores. En 2002, Donovan visitó a las tropas estadounidenses en Corea del Sur. Donovan firmó balones y fotografías.

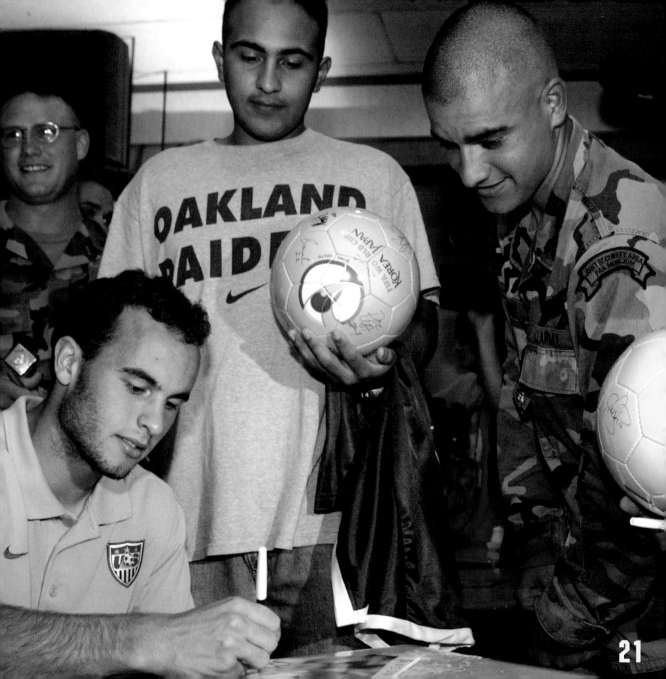

Glossary / Glosario

MLS (em el es) The Major League Soccer. The professional soccer league of the United States.

professional (pruh-**fesh**-nul) Somebody making money for doing something.

scorers (**skor**-erz) People who make goals.

World Cup (**wur**-uld **kup**) A soccer tournament that takes place every four years with teams from around the world.

Copa del Mundo (la) Competencia de fútbol, cada 4 años, en la que juegan los mejores equipos del mundo.

goleador Una persona que anota muchos goles en un partido o temporada.

MLS (la) Major League Soccer, liga de fútbol donde juegan los equipos profesionales de los Estados Unidos.

profesional Una persona que gana dinero realizando alguna actividad.

Resources / Recursos

Books in English/Libros en inglés

Buckley, James. Landon Donovan. Mankato: Child's World, 2006.

Books in Spanish/Libros en español

Page, Jason. El fútbol. Minneapolis: Two-Can Publishers, 2001

Web Sites

Due to the changing nature of Internet links, The Rosen Publishing Group has developed an online list of Web sites related to the subject of this book. This site is updated regularly. Please use this link to access the list:

www.buenasletraslinks.com/ss/donovan

Index

B
Bayer Leverkusen, 8
best player, 10

C
California, 4

E

Earthquakes, San
Jose, 12

G
Galaxy, Los Angeles,
14
Germany, 8
M
MLS, 12

W
World Cup, 10

Índice

A
Alemania, 8

B
Bayer Leverkusen, 8

C
California, 4
Copa del Mundo,
10

E
Earthquakes,
San José, 12

G
Galaxy, Los
Ángeles, 14

M
mejor jugador, 10
MLS, 12